Merdi SITUMONIKA MATONDO

Police Nationale confronts urban banditry in Kinshasa Police Nationale

Merdi SITUMONIKA MATONDO

Police Nationale confronts urban banditry in Kinshasa Police Nationale

The ineffectiveness of the National Police in the face of rising urban banditry in Kinshasa

ScienciaScripts

Imprint

Cover image: www.ingimage.com

This book is a translation from the original published under ISBN 978-3-639-56063-3.

Publisher:
Sciencia Scripts
is a trademark of
Dodo Books Indian Ocean Ltd. and OmniScriptum S.R.L publishing group

120 High Road, East Finchley, London, N2 9ED, United Kingdom
Str. Armeneasca 28/1, office 1, Chisinau MD-2012, Republic of Moldova, Europe
Managing Directors: Ieva Konstantinova, Victoria Ursu
info@omniscriptum.com

Printed at: see last page
ISBN: 978-620-6-77282-8

THE NATIONAL POLICE AND URBAN BANDITRY IN KINSHASA THE INEFFECTIVENESS OF THE NATIONAL POLICE IN THE FACE OF RISING URBAN BANDITRY IN KINSHASA

INTRODUCTION

The State claims a monopoly on legitimate violence within the territory of the Republic. Today, this formula is considered to be a characteristic and the very foundation of every modern state(1).

The police are therefore the main State apparatus responsible for exercising a monopoly on physical violence within the national territory. The police are the most visible manifestation of State authority and are responsible for public safety. It is therefore absolutely unacceptable for the police to be incapable of ensuring the safety of citizens.

For several years now, the Democratic Republic of Congo in general, and the city of Kinshasa in particular, have been living to the rhythm of criminal gangs. This phenomenon continues to grow in city of Kinshasa, and many Kinshasa residents complain about the inability of the police to deal with it, which raises the question of the causes of the ineffectiveness of the police in dealing with these criminal gangs. This situation raises the question of the ineffectiveness of the national police in dealing with the rise of urban banditry - the case of the Kuluna phenomenon in the city of Kinshasa. This is a thorny issue that requires particular attention in democratic political systems. The essential motivation behind this reflection is to advance the debate on the police response to this phenomenon in order to propose a genuine response to this situation.

However sensitive may be, the police in the DRC remain a mystified subject because of the various names given to them: state secret, defence secret, military secret, professional secret, which means that the public debate on this issue is not open to everyone. As a result, little work is directed towards this debate.

This leads us to ask the following questions: What explains these acts of misconduct? Why cant the national police force cope?

What went wrong in the various police operations?

What are the problems and challenges facing the national police?

What can be done about it?

In the Democratic Republic of Congo, the national police force is, in accordance with organic law no. 11 /013 of 11 August on the organisation and operation of the Congolese national police force, a public service that is civil, accessible, responsive to the population and responsible for security and safety. public tranquillity, the safety of people and their property, the maintenance and re-establishment of public order and the close protection of high authority. Unfortunately, today we realise that the national police force is incapable of dealing with urban banditry, commonly known as the kuluna phenomenon, which carries out acts of deviance that disturb the peace of the population. As a result, it is now imperative to put an end to these acts that are gangreneing Congolese society, through a genuine reform of the national police force and the creation of an anti-gang brigade. The persistence of these deviant acts by bandits commonly known as kuluna is due to a lack of organisation, insofar as the police and law enforcement officers are poorly recruited, as result of the poor recruitment policy which is crystallising and which is characterised in our country by fraud, corruption, clientelism, nepotism and tribalism. Poor working and living conditions, characterised by a lack of resources to carry out their duties, which crystallise in the protection of people and their property; and poor living and working conditions have resulted in increased corruption within the national police force. As a result of all this, there is an urgent need for a police recruitment policy that must respect the criteria set out in Article 185 of the Constitution, which stipulates that staffing at all levels, and command functions at all times and in all circumstances, must take account of objective criteria relating both aptitude and to the ability to carry out their duties. physical condition, good character and fair representation of the provinces. And by effectively combating anti-values such as fraud and corruption, but also by promoting meritocracy.The application of severe sanctions against police officers who engage in illegal or illicit practices, but also against officers who resort to clandestine recruitment of police officers so that this serves as an example to other officers or non-commissioned officers; the improvement of the living and working conditions of police officers so that they can carry out their duties in accordance with the law.

Hence the need to set up this brigade to remedy the situation, which is getting worse all the time in the city of Kinshasa.

In addition to the introduction, this work comprises two chapters. The first chapter deals with general information about the Police

Nationale (PN) divided into two sections: the history and missions of Police Nationale (section 1) and the organisation and operation of the Police Nationale (section 2). The second chapter looks at urban banditry in Kinshasa, its definition and history (section 1), the various causes (section 2), and the response of the National Police to this phenomenon.

CHAPTER I

GENERAL INFORMATION

This chapter contains two sections, the first focusing on the history of the police (section 1) and the second on the missions and functions of the national police (section 2).

Section .1. Historical background

§.1. History of the Police

Origin of the policy

Etymologically, the word police comes from the Latin word politia, which is the romanisation of the Greek word politeio meaning political regime, citizenship, administration, civil party and the word polis meaning city.
The term police refers generally to the activity ensuring the safety of people and property and maintaining public order by enforcing the law.
The history of the police traces the history of the police, an invention antiquity that developed in the cities of the Middle Ages, in fact, if Rome had enarchs responsible for monitoring morals, public discipline and the arrest of brigands. The police appeared in Italy and France in towns that retained their status as municipalities(2).
In ancient China, the maintenance of laws was devolved to "prefects" for thousands of years. The Chinese territory was divided into prefectures in the states of Chu and Jin during the spring and autumn periods. autumn (-722 to 481 BC). These officials were appointed by the local governor, who was himself answerable to the emperor. The prefects were a mixture civil administrators and police officers who reported offenders to the local magistrate, like a modern

judge, for trial. Prefects appointed sub-prefects to assist them administering the law and punishing crime. The concept of the prefecture gradually spread to neighbouring cultures such as Korea and Japan.

In ancient Greece, publicly-owned slaves were used by magistrates as policemen. In Athens, a group of 300 Scythian slaves were used to maintain order, control crowds and make arrests. Other functions, such as enquiries and investigations, were the responsibility of the citizens themselves[3].

Until its decline, the Roman Empire had a relatively effective system for maintaining order, although a real police force was never set up in the city of Rome itself. Many police tactics were inspired by the Greek police. Under the reign of Augustus (27 BC - 14 AD), the capital, almost reaching the size of the city, was reinforced by the Praetorian Guard from the 5th century onwards, and policing became a function of the clan and state chiefs.

In England, the first police force appeared in the time of King Alfred the Great (876-899) with the tything, which consisted of ten officers under the command of a chief constable. In Germany, the role of the police force was defined in the 15th century, before the enactment of the three imperial police laws a century later. In France, it was under Louis XIV that Colbert created the position of police lieutenant. It was an office paid to the royalty and which authorised its holder to control the units of measurement of the capital, Paris, before seeing its field of prerogatives extended over time.

B. History of the Congolese National Police

The police force in the Democratic Republic of Congo had its beginnings in the Force Publique (FP), which was created in 1886 by Camille COQUILHAT (from the name CoquilhatVille, now Province of Equateur, derives) when King Leopold II of Belgium, who had just taken possession of the country, the Etat Indépendant du Congo (EIC), ordered his Minister of Internal Affairs to create a

Military and Police Force[4].

1. The Public Force (PF)

The public force had played dual role: military force and police force.
In 1887 it had 14,000 men:

✓ 8,000 natives from annual collections ;

✓ 4,000 Congolese volunteers and

✓ 2,000 foreign volunteers.

From 1886 to 1908, the officer corps consisted of:

✓ 648 Belgians ;

✓ 192 Italians ;

✓ 53 Danish ;

✓ 47 Swedish ;

✓ 26 Norwegian and

✓ a smaller number recruited from other countries such as the United Kingdom and the United States.

After the Belgian government took over the Independent State of Congo in 1908, the Force Publique was organised into 21 separate companies, supplemented by artillery and engineering units. Each company comprised at least 4 white officers, 8 Congolese non-commissioned officers and more than 150 soldiers. These Belgian officers quickly took the place of the Europeans of all origins who made up the autonomous force of 6 companies and a cycling unit. In 1914, the PS comprised around 17,000 soldiers, including the Katangese forces included. Most served in small garrisons assigned to a territory, with a police role; only the Katangese units were organised into battalions, with a primary military function. Efforts were made to remedy the excesses of the EIC period and to transform the FP into a more traditional, better-disciplined colonial force. Their weaponry differed somewhat from that of the Belgian army. The Albini-braendlin 11mm rifle was the individual weapon, while Maxim machine guns and cannons (Nordenfeld 4.7 cm and Krupp 7.5 cm) supported the infantry. Soldiers continued to wear a blue uniform with a red light, replaced by a khaki uniform for the period of 1915 - 1917. Annual enlistment was based a quota system of recruits (volunteers and non-volunteers) set by district, with non-volunteers automatically designated by village chiefs, and lasted for 7 years. In 1953, the total strength of the police force was 22,416 men and the contingent to be recruited that year was 3,788 men. In 1956, out of a recruitment contingent of 3,814 men, there were 1,544 volunteers, 1,426 re-enlisted soldiers and only 849 militiamen drawn by lot or designated by their tribal chiefs. On 28 September 1959, a school for warrant officers was created and opened its doors to 9 elite Congolese officers who, until that date, could not rise above the rank of first sergeant major. At independence, there were only 20 African cadets.

2. The National Police

Territorial service troops (the PS's police structure) were established by the decree of 10 May 1919. These troops were distributed among the various provincial territories according to need and placed under the authority of territorial chiefs. Later, in 1959, these troops were transformed into gendarmerie units[5]. In 1966, the DRC's national police force reported to the Minister of the Interior. It numbered around 25,000 men and its mission was to maintain public order and security in towns and rural areas[6]. By presidential decree of 3 July 1972, the national gendarmerie was created from the merger of the national police and the Gendarmerie (dissolved by the same decree-law of 31 July 1972), hence the name Gendarmerie Nationale ;

3. The National Gendarmerie

The National Gendarmerie was created by Law No. 72/031 of 31 July 1972, which established the National Gendarmerie (Gend Nat). It was placed under the authority of the Ministry of Defence by the Ordinance-Law of 31 July integrating elements of the Gendarmerie Nationale into the Zairian armed forces, of which it made up just over half the total strength. When it was created, it numbered around 21,000 men, and its mission was also to maintain and re-establish public order and carry out judicial police missions. It was subdivided into two components, following the Belgian model of the time:

- Territorial Gendarmerie, which retained the same missions as the former national police and
- The Mobile Gendarmerie, which was a para-military force capable of transforming itself into an infantry unit (ground force) in

It should protect the country against external aggression, and support territorial gendarmerie units in the event of major threats to public order and safety. Towards the end of the 1970s, the gendarmerie numbered around 30,000 men, spread across nine Circonscriptions (Circo), i.e. one "Circo" per region (province) of the country. [7] Towards the 1980s, the deplorable training, supervision and living conditions, as well as the limited operational capacity of the gendarmes, made it difficult and often ineffective for them to carry out their missions. It was during this period that Mobutu doubled the number of gendarmes by creating the Garde Civile (Gaci), a praetorian para-military force specialised in border policing and operating between the army and the national gendarmerie, depending on the interests of its leaders.In addition to these tasks of administering prisons and military districts, the Zairian national gendarmerie special services such as the mobile brigade and the special research and surveillance brigade.

4. The Civil Guard

The Civil Guard was created by Ordinance-Law N 84/036 of 28 August 1984, which created and organised the Civil Guard. The main mission of the Civil Guard was to combat terrorism and protect the national borders.

The Guardia Civil was a paramilitary police force strong of 10,000 well-equipped, trained and maintained men. The latter excelled particularly in the posts borders, that the gendarmerienational resta especially active in the areas and rural areas. [8]

The Civil Guard had specialised elite units on its payroll, including : Rapid Intervention Forces (FIRA) ;

Special Border Brigade, Guard Brigade, Dog Brigade; Search Brigade; Anti-Riot Unit; Anti-Terrorist Unit;

Unité de Morale, Unité Territoriale, etc.

They were to become infamous for their numerous acts of violence and looting during the political protests that followed Mobutu's downfall.

In Zaire, the role of the judicial police was assigned to the national gendarmerie and the civil guard. As a result, all officers and non-commissioned officers of the national gendarmerie and the military provost marshal's office, as well as members of the civil guard, were Officers of the Judicial Police with General Jurisdiction (OPJ/CG).

5. Congolese National Police

The national police force that we had before the reform was created by the late president Mzée Laurent désiré Kabila in GOMA on 22 April 1997 during the advance of the Alliance des Forces Démocratiques pour la Libération du Congo (AFDL), a de facto creation and not a legal one, with no legal text organising it for 5 years. It was not until 2002, under the reign of his son, President Joseph

Kabila Kabange, and through decree-law N 002-2002 on the institution, organisation and functioning of the Congolese National Police and the same decree dissolving the national gendarmerie and the civil guard, that the Congolese National Police was created.

5.1. Tasks of the PNC under the Decree-Law of N°002-2002

The PNC is responsible for public safety and tranquillity, the safety of people and their property, the maintenance and restoration public order and the close protection of senior figures in accordance with the law on the Congolese national police force[9].

The missions of the national police force are both preventive and repressive. They are divided into ordinary and extraordinary missions. Ordinary missions are those that are carried out on a daily basis or at specific times, without the need any requisition from the authorities. Extraordinary missions are those that are carried out only by virtue of requisitions or requests for assistance. Special missions are those that are carried out to deputise for, support or assist services specially set up for this purpose. In the context of special missions, police officers national can be seconded to specialist bodies.

1. Ordinary missions

The Congolese national police force is responsible for preventing offences, investigating them and apprehending the perpetrators in manner and forms provided for by law. It ensures that the laws and regulations of the Republic are respected and enforced. It searches for and seizes persons caught in flagrante delicto or pursued by public clamour; it also searches for persons whose arrest has been legally ordered and makes them available to the competent authority.

Without prejudice to the provisions of the law, the national police force will also detain, for the time necessary to verify their identity, any person whose behaviour appears suspicious or who is walking around without identity . The national police force will seize intoxicated persons who wander onto the public highway and put them out of their misery in the cases and forms provided for by law.The national police force prevents dangerous lunatics from wandering, seizes them and immediately hands them over to the competent civil authority. It acts in the same way with regard to those reported to it as having escaped from institutions for the insane. The national police record the discovery of any individual found dead. It notifies the administrative and judicial authorities. The national police are responsible for policing traffic. It maintains communications and free passage at all times and ensures free movement. The national police force public peace and quiet at all times. To this end, they stay within range of large gatherings and keep an eye on them. They report any unauthorised gatherings to the administrative authorities(10).

The national police disperse on the initiative of :

- any armed gathering;
- any unarmed gathering attempting to free prisoners or convicts, endangering life or limb, or invading, pillaging or destroying property;

- armed assemblies opposing the execution of the law, a judgement or a constraint;
- assemblies formed in contravention of a regulation or police order.

In the event of a major disaster or incident, such as flooding, breaching of dykes or fire, the national police will go to the scene and notify the relevant administrative and judicial authorities.

Pending the intervention of these authorities, it shall take appropriate measures to save individuals in danger, protect the evacuation of people and property and prevent looting. The personal service of residents may be required. They are required to comply with these requisitions. and to provide all means of transport and all other objects necessary to rescue people and preserve property. Refusal to comply with these requisitions is punishable in accordance with the legal provisions in force.[11] The national police force will only leave the scene once it is satisfied that its presence is no longer required to protect property, maintain public peace and arrest the perpetrators of offences that may have directly or indirectly caused the disaster or incident.

The national police force carries out its ordinary duties as set out this decree-law, in particular during rounds, patrols, searches and in the bush. These various services are organised in such a way that all the places under their coverage are regularly monitored.

In the course of their duties, the police shall obtain information from the local authorities and from any reliable person on any offences that may have been committed, on facts likely to disturb public order, on the place of retreat of individuals reported or pursued by public clamour, as well as on any fact likely to undermine public order and State security.[12]

The events that require special reports to be drawn up and sent fall into the following categories:

- An event that has the character of a real disaster and requires prompt and decisive action, either to rescue people or to protect people and property, such as floods, landslides, railway accidents, shipwrecks, explosions and fires;
- events of serious importance from the point of view of public order or State security and requiring special measures to maintain order, such as strikes, popular riots, anarchic attacks, plots, incitement to revolt, the discovery arms or ammunition depots clandestine explosives workshops;

- offences which, either because of their frequency or the circumstances in which they occurred, or because of the nature of the persons involved, have aroused emotion or concern in the regions or require special measures, such as acts of banditry or attacks on public officials;

- Acts and manoeuvres affecting national defence, such as espionage, attacks on posts or sentries, inciting police or military personnel to indiscipline or desertion.

2. Special missions

The national police force is specifically responsible for the guarding and security of the heads of the constituted bodies as well as VIPs. The national police force is responsible for all forms of anti-terrorist operations. The national police shall assist the relevant specialised bodies and services in the surveillance of points of entry into the national territory, in search of illegal immigrants and usurpers of Congolese nationality[13]. The national police participate in the fight against fraud, smuggling, poaching, corruption and theft of precious substances by providing support and assistance to the relevant specialised bodies and services. It assists mining companies in protecting their assets. The national police force supports environmental and nature conservation initiatives by providing support and assistance to the relevant specialist bodies and services.

The national police force apprehends any soldier who breaks the law. On receiving a wanted notice, it will pursue any soldier who has deserted or is unlawfully absent from his unit; it will take the measures prescribed by the law and regulations of the Republic. In all cases, it informs the commander of the unit to which the soldier concerned belongs and, at the request of the government, the national police collaborate in the measures taken to ensure the mobilisation of the army and participate in the defence of the integrity of the territory.

5.2. The organisation and operation of the PNC under Decree-Law of 2002

A. Structures

The Congolese national police included :

- a National Police High Council;

- a national police inspectorate;

- provincial inspectorates of the national police.

1. central structure

a. The National Police High Council

The Conseil supérieur de la police nationale is a deliberative, advisory and disciplinary body. It is chaired by the Minister referred to in article 4 or his delegate. The following are members of the Conseil supérieur de la Police nationale in a deliberative and consultative capacity:

- the Inspector General of the National Police;
- Deputy Inspectors General ;
- directors and heads of central services;
- the commanders of large units;
- provincial inspectors.
- Its members sit disciplinary matters:
- the Inspector General of the National Police;

- Deputy Inspectors General;
- the Human Resources Director;
- the directors or commanders concerned by the matters to be examined;
- the provincial inspector responsible for the officer being prosecuted.

b. National Police Inspectorate

The national police force is under the command a senior national police officer known as the Inspector General of the National Police, assisted by two Deputy Inspectors General:

- a deputy inspector general in charge of intelligence and operations;
- a deputy inspector general in charge of administration and logistics[14]

The Inspector General of the National Police and the Deputy Inspectors General are appointed and, if necessary, relieved of their duties by the President of the Republic.

The Inspector General of the National Police commands and supervises all national police forces in accordance with the laws and regulations of the Republic in force. It is responsible for its management, personnel and financial resources, as well as the current and future movable and immovable property made available to the national police force.

He is responsible for drawing up and implementing the national police budget. He is the head of the national police force and is responsible for its operations. In this capacity, he represents the national police force in dealings with the public authorities and third parties. The Inspector General is assisted a cabinet.

The Deputy Inspectors General assist the Inspector General in his duties, each within his own remit.[15] However, they are responsible for all other matters that may be delegated to them by the Inspector General with subsequent signature, or supervise one or more other sectors that the Inspector General may entrust to them.

In the event of absence or incapacity, the Inspector General of the National Police shall be replaced by one of the Deputy Inspectors General in the order of their appointment. Each Deputy Inspector General assists the Inspector General in supervising one or more departments according to his or her specific remit. The Inspectorate General of the National Police comprised the following central departments:

- human resources;
- general intelligence and special services;
- organisation, training and operations;
- logistics;
- public relations and press;
- technical services: communications: engineering and health;
- research and IT management;
- budget and finance;
- The following central special services:
- intendance-générale;
- school inspectorate;
- medical service;

The large units below:

- the national legion of rapid intervention police (P.I.R.);
- the guard brigade;
- An academy;
- Schools;
- Training centres[16]

2. Provincial structures

a. Provincial inspectorates of the national police

In each province, the national police force is organised into a Provincial Inspectorate under the command a Provincial Commander. provincial inspector of the national police, assisted by a deputy provincial inspector. The Provincial Inspector of the National Police and the Deputy Provincial Inspector are appointed and, if necessary, relieved of their duties by the President of the Republic[17].

A. The units

The units within the Congolese national police force were organised as follows: On the one hand, there were units attached directly to the Inspectorate General, known as large units, and on the other, units attached to each provincial inspectorate. The main units of the Congolese national police are :

- The national legion of rapid intervention police (P.I.R.);
- The guard brigade.

At provincial level, the units were distributed as follows:

- territorial units;
- intervention units;
- specialised units or services.

The territorial units are established in accordance with the administrative subdivision of the national territory or in proportion to the demographic and territorial importance of the entities concerned.

The territorial units of provincial inspectorate of the national police are

- the police district for the district;
- the police station for the area or municipality;
- the police sub-station for the community.[18] The intervention units are organically divided into:

- brigade;
- battalion or group;
- company;
- peloton;
- section.

The specialised units and services of the provincial inspectorates of the national police include

- criminal police (anti-gang, anti-fraud, drugs, etc.);
- the rolling policy;

- the mining police;
- river, lake and maritime policing[19]

C. The different ranks within the Congolese national police force

The ranks of the Congolese national police were classified into six categories:

a. Divisional inspectors

- The Chief Divisional Inspector ;

- The Divisional Inspector ;

- The Deputy Divisional Inspector.

b. The inspectors

- Chief Inspector ;

- Inspector;

- The deputy inspector.

c. The commissioners

- Lead Commissioner ;

- Commissioner;

- Deputy Commissioner.

d. The deputy commissioners

- principal deputy commissioner ;

- sub-commissioner ;

- deputy commissioner.

e. Brigadiers

- Chief Brigadier ;

- Brigadier ;

- Deputy Brigadier[20]

f. Police officers

- Senior police officer ;

- Police officer ;

- Assistant police officer.Section 2. The National Police under Organic Law No. 11/O13 of 11 August 2011

§ 1 Functions and Missions

A. The NP has two functions :

The Administrative Function, responsible for prevention, and the Judicial Function, responsible for enforcement.

B. Missions of PN

The missions of the Congolese National Police are both preventive and repressive. They are carried out in the context of territorial surveillance and ensuring the safety of the population. Its missions are subdivided into ordinary, extraordinary and special missions.

a) Ordinary missions

Ordinary duties are carried out as part of normal police service. Their purpose is to prevent public order disturbances and offences, to record them, to gather evidence, to search for and identify the perpetrators and to bring them before the competent judicial authority.

They are carried out on a daily basis without the need for a requisition from the authorities[21].

Ordinary tasks include

- General information ;The fight against crime ;
- The fight against terrorism ;
- Combating violence and monitoring and protecting children;
- Road safety, communication and transport routes ;
- Helping the population in the event of disaster;
- Safeguarding public health and hygiene ;

b)Extraordinary Missions

Extraordinary missions are those that can only be carried out by virtue of a written requisition issued by the administrative or judicial authorities.

To this end, NP staff are required, under penalty of punishment, to comply promptly with any lawful request from these authorities.

c) Special missions

Special missions are those that are carried out according to circumstances, as a substitute, in support of or in conjunction with other services.

§ 2. Structures

The National Police is made up of :

- The Police High Council ;
- The General Commissariat ;
- The Inspectorate General ;
- Provincial Commissariats

- Territorial and local units

A. National structures

1. The Police High Council

The Supreme Police Council is an advisory body to the government on police and security matters[22].

The Police High Council gives its opinion on all matters relating to the general regulations, training and reinforcement of staff, discipline, careers and remuneration of national police personnel[23].

The Police High Council is made up of :

✓ the minister for the interior ;

✓ the minister for justice ;

✓ the Commissioner General of Police ;

✓ Inspector General of Police;

✓ the Deputy General Commissioners ;

✓ the Director General of Police Training Schools;

✓ Provincial Commissioners.

It has a permanent secretariat, the head of which, having at least the rank of senior commissioner or senior police officer, is appointed, relieved of his duties and, if necessary, dismissed by the President of the Republic, on the basis of a government proposal discussed in the Council Ministers, after consulting the Supreme Defence Council[(24)].

The Superior Police Council may call upon the expertise of any person in the study of matters submitted to it. The Board of Governors shall meet in ordinary session every six months and whenever necessary, at the call of its Chairman.[25] It is chaired by the Minister for Home Affairs.

2. The General Commissariat

The General Commissariat is a command structure. It is headed by a General Commissioner.[26] The Commissioner General is a Divisional Commissioner. He is assisted by three deputies in the category of Divisional Commissioner, responsible for administrative policing, judicial policing and support and management.[27] The Commissioner General and his deputies shall be appointed, relieved of their duties and, where appropriate, dismissed, by order of the President of the Republic on a proposal from the Government deliberated in the Council of Ministers, after hearing the opinion of the Supreme Defence Council[28]. The General Commissioner has the following responsibilities:

- Apply and enforce all legal provisions relating to the tasks assigned to the national police force;
- Supervise the smooth running of the central directorates, central services, specialised national units and provincial police stations;
- To ensure a harmonious relationship between the executives and other officers of the administrative police, the judicial police and those of support and management;
- Submit a monthly report on the development of the national police force to the Minister for Home Affairs;
- Submit a monthly report to the Minister of Justice on developments in crime and human rights;
- Maintaining the discipline and morale of national police personnel;
- Ensuring the recruitment, periodic training and promotion of personnel in accordance with national police staff regulations;
- Supervise and control the operation of all expenditure or cash outflows and draw up the annual budget;
- Supervising and controlling the operation of the National Police Academy and

Schools;

- Monitoring international police cooperation;

- To exercise all other powers conferred on it by the Constitution, laws and regulations.

The Commissioner General may, in financial matters, delegate his powers to one of his deputies and to the Provincial Commissioners.[29] It has its .

The number of members of the Private Office may not exceed fifteen.[30] The Commissioner General may entrust his deputies with any other tasks and delegate their signature.

If he is absent or unable to act, he is replaced by the most senior Deputy General Commissioner in accordance with his appointment.

Under the authority of the Commissioner General, the Deputy Commissioner General in charge of the administrative police coordinates the activities that contribute to carrying out the preventive missions of the national police.[31]

As part of this role, it is responsible for the following tasks in particular:

- Operational coordination of ordinary, extraordinary and special missions of the administrative police, directorates and central services;

- Operational coordination of the provincial administrative police departments ;

- Coordinating the fight against gender-based violence and monitoring and protecting children;

- Monitoring the national police force's general intervention reserve.

Under the authority of the Commissioner General, the Deputy Commissioner General in charge of the Judicial Police coordinates the activities that contribute to carrying out the law enforcement missions of the national police force.[32]

Within this framework, the Deputy Commissioner General in charge of the Judicial Police is responsible for the following tasks in particular:

- Using the information needed to public action ;
- Supervision and coordination of judicial police missions ;
- Operational coordination of the provincial criminal investigation departments ;
- Technical and forensic police control ;
- The control of the National Central Bureau-INTERPOL ;
- Monitoring international police cooperation ;
- Control of the central database

The Deputy Commissioner General in charge of support and management coordinates, under the authority of the Commissioner General, the activities involved in carrying out the support and management missions of the national police force.
In this role, you will be responsible for the following tasks:

- Participating in the drafting of pre-projects on the organisation and internal workings of the national police force and in studies relating the support of police missions and responsibilities;
- Drawing up the preliminary draft annual budget;
- Planning and managing the recruitment, use, remuneration and career of police personnel;
- Provide other departments with the resources of all kinds that are essential to their operation;
- Ensure the coordination of directorates support and management departments.

The General Commissioner comprises :

- Central departments, central services central services and specialised national units ;
- The Directorate-General for Schools and Training[33]

The central directorates and specialised national units responsible for the administrative police are :

- Direction de la sécurité publique ;
- Direction des renseignements généraux ;
- Directorate of Civil Protection ;
- Border Police Directorate ;
- River, Lake, Maritime and Railways Communication Department;
- Institutions and VIPs Protection Unit ;
- National Police Intervention Legion.

The directorates and departments of the Judicial Police are :

- Directorate of Technical and Scientific Police ;
- Crime Control Department ;
- Telecommunications and New Technologies Department ;
- Directorate for Combating Economic and Financial Crime ;
- Drugs Directorate ;
- Criminal Investigation Department and Central Index ;
- National Central Bureau-INTERPOL ;
- Statistics department[34]

Departments and central services responsible support and management are :

- Human Resources Department ;

- Budget and Finance Department ;

- Logistics department ;

- Infrastructure management and maintenance department ;

- Communications and Telecommunications Service; Health Service ;
- Social Affairs Department ;

- IT services ;

- Chaplaincies.

The following Directorates and Central Services report to the Commissioner General:
- Research and Planning Department ;

- Information and communication services ;

- International police cooperation services.

Central Directors, heads of central services and commanders of specialised national units and their deputies shall be appointed, relieved of their duties and, where appropriate, dismissed by Order of the President of the Republic on a proposal from the Government. deliberated by the Council of Ministers, after hearing the opinion of the Supreme Defence Council.
The Directorate General of Schools and Training is responsible for designing and implementing initial, in-service and specialist training for national police personnel.
The Directorate General of Schools and Training draws up the training master plan in accordance with the guidelines laid down by the Police High Council. There is also the Legal and Litigation Department, which is also attached to the Police Headquarters.

3. The Inspectorate General

The Inspectorate General is responsible for monitoring, auditing, investigating and evaluating the services and units of the national police force, under the authority of the Minister of the Interior and Home Affairs[35].

It supervises the organisation and operation of the national police force.[36] The Inspectorate General is responsible for ensuring that the laws and regulations of the Republic are strictly applied by the staff of the national police force, as well as the directives and instructions relating to the proper operation of the force, in particular :

- Assessing respect for fundamental rights, human rights and the protection of individual and collective freedoms in the performance of police duties;
- Controlling the rational management of human resources and national police services ;Monitoring the application of the gender principle in appointments and postings within the national police force ;
- Controlling pay and implementation of the budget allocated to the national police force ;
- Checking the suitability and reliability equipment and infrastructure;
- Assessing the performance and operational and administrative capabilities of police units and services;
- Monitoring and assessment of training ;
- Monitoring the implementation of the national police code of ethics.

The Inspectorate General is headed by an Inspector General in the category of Chief Inspector.[37]

The Inspector General is assisted by two deputies in the category of divisional commissioners. The Inspector General has an office.

Under the direction of the Inspector General, the Deputy Inspectors General are responsible respectively for control, audit, investigation, evaluation and support and management.

The Inspector General and his deputies shall be appointed, relieved of their duties and, where appropriate, dismissed, by Order of the President of the Republic on a proposal from the Government discussed in the Council of Ministers, after hearing the Supreme Defence Council.

B. Provincial structures

1. The Provincial Commissariat

The Provincial Commissariat is a command structure for police units in each province. It reports to the General Commissariat and is placed under the authority a Provincial Commissioner in the category of Divisional Commissioner, assisted by three Deputy Provincial Commissioners in the category of Senior Commissioner, who are responsible for administrative policing, judicial policing and support and management respectively.[38] Each Commissariat is responsible for ensuring that administrative policing, judicial policing and support and management activities are carried out properly.[39]

The Provincial Commissioner and his deputies are appointed, relieved their duties and, if necessary, dismissed by Ordinance of the President of the Republic on a proposal from the Government deliberated in the Council of Ministers, after hearing the Supreme Defence Council[40].

2. Local territorial units and

Territorial and local units are set up in accordance with the administrative subdivision of the national territory and according to security needs.

C. The different ranks within the national police force

The national police force has six categories of ranks, distributed as follows:[41]

- Category A1: Divisional Police Commissioners;

- Category A2: Senior Police Commissioners;

- Category B: Police Commissioners;

- Category C: Deputy Police Commissioners;

- Category D: Police Brigadiers;

- Category E: Police officers.

The Divisional Commissioners category comprises four categories grades :

- Chief Divisional Commissioner ;

- Senior Divisional Commissioner ;

- Divisional Commissioner ;

- Deputy Divisional Commissioner.

The category of senior police commissioner comprises three grades:

- Senior Chief Commissioner ;

- Senior commissioner ;

- Deputy Commissioner ;

The Police Commissioner category comprises three grades:

- Lead Commissioner ;

- Commissioner;

- Deputy Commissioner.

The Police Brigadier category comprises three grades:

- Chief Brigadier ;

- Brigadier first class ;

- Brigadier.

The Police Officer category comprises three grades:

- Senior police officer ;

- Police officer first class ;

- Second-class police officer[42]

CHAPTER 2

URBAN BANDITRY IN KINSHASA

Section 1: Background and definition

A. History

Urban banditry in Kinshasa, commonly known as the kuluna phenomenon, has taken a very worrying rise. The insecurity caused by these criminal gangs continues to grow in the city of Kinshasa. These bandits have been around since the year 2000. But it was around 2005 that the gangs began to grow. Some authors explain the genesis of this phenomenon by confrontations between young people called pomba, i.e. sportsmen who consider themselves strong because of their practice of martial arts. To challenge each other, these young pomba grouped together in what were then known as "stables" (gangs or clubs) would confront pomba from rival stables in the public square in very violent brawls. This fuelled resentment on both sides, so much so that members of rival gangs who ventured to cross the territory of the opposing neighbourhood were violently attacked.[43]

These clashes created an atmosphere of terror, with many collateral victims in the neighbourhoods hosting the duels. The youngsters took advantage of the chaos to steal, pillage, extort, even rape and kill... These barbaric acts earned these youngsters, organised in gangs, the name kuluna. Youth gangs first appeared on the city's streets in the 1950s. Known as the Bills or Yankees, they brought juvenile violence to the townships of Kinshasa.[44]

Later, as the political and economic decline triggered by the regime of former president Mobuto Sese Seko in the 1990s progressed, young unemployed people from the Congolese countryside who had come to the city to find work took over the urban areas. As the country sank into an unprecedented economic crisis, they took to the streets in a desperate attempt to survive.

The Kuluna emerged as a social phenomenon around year 2000against a backdrop of the collapse of the state and public order.3 During this period of anarchy and civil war, they operated in the streets of the poorest districts of Kinshasa, such as Yolo, Limete, Matete and Makala. Since then, despite several crackdowns on them by the police, their influence has spread to the rest of the city but also, as mentioned above, to other towns[45].

From the suburbs of Kinshasa where the police did not dare to venture, the gangs have gradually moved into the central districts as well as the military and police camps, even recruiting their members from among the children of officers. "You know, here, the children of the PNC [Congolese National Police] are all Kuluna", said a resident of Lingwala, a commune of Kinshasa. Today, with the exception of Gombe in the centre of town, where the The Kuluna gangs can be found everywhere in the capital, including the ministries and embassies, but in greater numbers in the poor/slum areas (Lingwala, Barumbu, etc.) and in deprived central districts such as Kasa Vubu, Ngiri Ngiri, Kalamu, Bumbu, Makala and Limete. They can also be found in military camps such as Muganga, N'Djili, Kimbanseke, Masina and Ceta. In their operations, they tend to defend their territory. A neighbourhood, if it is part of one, "belongs" to them - they attack strangers who pass through it but do not attack those who live there. Several gangs may cohabit in the same neighbourhood, a system of governance allowing them to establish a hierarchy based on their reputation and the violence they display - the best-known groups, for their part, "sponsor" the gangs. "Those that have formed more recently. What's more, every neighbourhood has a number of small, unknown Kuluna gangs; only those that have been established for some time have made a name for themselves and are able to control a territory.Anyone wishing to join a Kuluna gang must prove their strength and fighting skills. Put to the test for a time, candidates are subjected to violence imposed on them by the elders6 and have to perform services for the organisation (supplying alcohol, drugs, etc.). To earn the respect a gang leader and a place in his entourage, they have to attack and injure rival gang members. "I wanted to be strong and respected, so I became Kuluna. Because I was good at fighting, I managed to join [the gang]. "explained a member of one of these groups. Gang fights are an essential part of the Kuluna way of life, almost as important as their criminal activities: winning the respect of other gangs is vital to them. As night falls, the streets of Kinshasa's shantytowns become the scene of violent clashes between young criminals. The gangs also form alliances, which often fluctuate wildly (just like the gangs themselves).[46]

B. Definition

From the Lingala verb kolona, meaning "to plant" or "to cultivate". Derived from the French word "colonisateur", "Kuluna" also has its origins in the military term "colonne", which refers to a formation of troops in close order as opposed to a line. First used in the 1990s to refer to urban youths from the south-west of the DRC entering Angola illegally from the north in search of diamonds, the term has become a generic way of referring to criminals since 2000. Today, it is used in specific expressions to identify certain categories of criminals. For example, Kuluna in white collar and Kuluna in tie refer to business criminals, and Kuluna in uniform refers to police and military officers involved in extortion.[47]

In Lingala, the local language spoken in the Congolese capital, the term "kuluna" does not exist. Of all the people we met, only two managed to explain the origin of the term. And they were two officers of the Congolese national police It's a term borrowed from the Portuguese language (from Angola). In

Portuguese, 'coluna' means 'band', 'column' or, according to the Petit Robert, 'group of individuals advancing one behind the other'. This was a reference to the disturbances caused by elements of Unita (the Union for the Total Independence of Angola), the political-military party led by Jonas Malero Savimbi. During the Angolan war (1975-2002), when elements of this rebel army burst into a region controlled by government forces, they terrorised, pillaged and ravaged everything in their path. It was by analogy with this indiscriminate violence that young Congolese returning from Angola, where they had been illegally mining diamonds in these war zones, described the operations of these gangs of young Kinshasa people as kuluna. The term is currently used to designate the perpetrators of these looting, extortion and violence operations throughout the city. It is not restricted to the Pomba. It encompasses different categories of people who have in common the fact that they are young, mostly with little schooling, idle and delinquent, acting in gangs. In the past, young people from the stables used to challenge each other honour, but in recent years, their 'descendants', the Kuluna, are no longer venting their violence solely on their counterparts who are also their rivals. Ordinary citizens, street vendors and passers-by have become the victims of a barbarity aimed at robbing them of the valuables in their possession (smartphones, jewellery, cash, etc.). So they sometimes reproduce the modus operandi of the stables by simulating a fight between themselves in a busy public place where there are salesmen or women. In the heat of the moment, they and other passers-by will try to escape in a hurry without having time to deal with the items for sale that they have spread out on the ground or on a small table. Some members of the group may then take advantage of the imbroglio to steal quietly (Shomba Kinyamba, 2015a, p. 38). The word Kuluna means both a band of outlaws and an uncontrollable young person identified as such. Etymologically, the word derives from Portuguese-Angolan[1]. Kuluna is a form of threat practised in the city of Kinshasa, which initially victimised young people aged between 5 and

17. Today, we are seeing a chronology of ages, and there is even talk of older people aged between 30 and 35 being the perpetrators of this evil. A Kuluna is a character categorised as threatening, like all criminals whose aim is to steal and harm with bladed weapons (cuffs, knives, stones) weak, unarmed people, often each other and even elderly people (grandparents), and even public authorities fall victim to their crimes. The Kulunas are the successors to the Pombas, the former name of the delinquents who, since the mid-2000s in Kinshasa, have been robbing, extorting money and easily injuring or cutting off their victims' arms with the machetes they are armed with, or even killing them outright in the face of resistance. Although infamous, the Kuluna have rarely been studied. Most of the information about them comes from the Congolese media, which focus on the violence perpetrated by their members and community discontent with urban crime and police responses. Because of this specific perspective, the press gives little insight into the gangs or their way of life. The Kuluna have forged criminal partnerships with members of the police and various political parties - a reality that the government is seeking to put an end to with violent political responses.

Section 2. The different causes

The causes include unemployment, drug use, parental poverty, feelings of insecurity and revenge.

§1 Unemployment and drug use

1. Unemployment

In the Democratic Republic of Congo, the rich are getting richer and the poor are getting poorer, making it inevitable that the poor, who are the victims of this economic injustice, will revolt. Unemployment is one of the main causes of the vulnerability of Congolese youth, and is a factor in the "Kuluna" phenomenon. Several Kulunas claim that they became involved in crime for economic reasons. They were forced to try and make a living by sowing suffering among the population, without which they cannot survive.[48]

Some of them are real men with wives and children to support at all costs. Apart from these assaults, the Kulunas have no other way of earning a living[5].

As a result, the Kulunas appear to be victims of the economic apartheid that characterises the Democratic Republic of Congo (DRC). The inequitable distribution of national wealth leads to frustration among the majority of the population, who feel that they are on the margins of the country without hope. In the history of countries, the confiscation of national wealth has always led to revolt by the victims of this social injustice[7]. In other words, the problem is good governance, which must eradicate the economic segregation of which young people are the majority victims.

In this sense, it can be said that the State itself creates an environment conducive to insecurity thanks to its poor economic system. The city of Kinshasa is one of the African cities where buildings are sprouting up like mushrooms and the latest brands of luxury vehicles are going from strength to strength, while the State budget is the lowest in Africa. This means that the wealth of the State is shared between a group of individuals who benefit from the privileges of public power and who have adopted financial embezzlement as their mode of government, behaving like real businessmen. The Kuluna phenomenon is a reaction citizens wronged by an unjust society. Thus, even in their modus operandi, the Kulunas do not attack a person who looks miserable. They must notice signs of wealth (jewellery, bulging pockets, the public exchange of foreign currency, etc.) on an individual before attacking him[8].

2. Drug use

As well as the economically motivated Kulunas, there is another category of Kulunas who have joined through training. This is the case of those who, without necessarily being forced to become radicalised criminals in order to survive, have joined the group by taking drugs with the Kulunas. By associating with criminals, you end up becoming a criminal yourself. This group is made up of young people whose parents are capable of taking care of them, but who choose to go outside the law. They are even sought out by their parents, who sometimes have them arrested for re-education in prison with a view to their social integration. They are, in a way, child prodigies who have left the family home for no good reason. For this group, crime is considered a distraction, a hobby, not a profession[49].

§2 Parents' poverty, feelings insecurity and revenge

A. Poverty among parents

Parental poverty is one of the main causes of family abandonment, leading heads of families (fathers) to shirk their family obligations look after and educate their children. Once again, it is poor economic governance that is responsible for the galloping parental poverty of Congolese parents. Since the time of Zairianisation, when businesses were expropriated from experienced white managers and given to novice Zairians, many businesses have gone bankrupt, leaving many parents unemployed. The looting of the 1990s wiped out the rest of what could be described as the national economy, leaving many unemployed parents with no job to look after their children. This shows that the Kulunas are victims of the State, itself a victim of predatory management.

It is also important to highlight the contribution of so-called revivalist churches to the destabilisation of families in Kinshasa. Competing with pubs terms of growth in numbers, the revivalist churches are at the root of the break-up of several witchcraft families, through gratuitous accusations against children, leading parents to get rid of . Among , the contribution of Spiritual Warfare Ministry of "Mama Olangi" can be highlighted with its famous examination of state of mind. This practice has led hundreds of thousands children to take to the streets and end up as Kulunas. in their quest for survival. This practice by churches should therefore be combated, given that the law on child protection guarantees the protection of children's rights.[50]

B. Feelings of insecurity and revenge

The young people whose testimonies we took explained that they chose to join the Kuluna to punish criminals and delinquents and to protect themselves and their loved ones - a desire for revenge born out of a perceived lack of justice and punishment. Paradoxically, self-defence and a sense of justice play a part in their decision to join a gang. Although Kinshasa has particularly high rates of poverty, it was not this factor that respondents attributed their enlistment to, but rather anger, injustice and frustration. For many young men, becoming a Kuluna gives them a sense of security and justice that they feel the Congolese authorities are unable to provide. Another decisive factor is pride in belonging to a Kuluna gang. Being part of a gang that ranks high in the Kuluna hierarchy can be seen as a sign of personal achievement and confer a certain social status in the shanty town concerned.

Section 3. The police response

§ 1. previous responses

We can divide this into 5 periods

1)From 2002

2)The year 2003

3)The year 2004

4)The year 2013

5)From 2020

This section looks at the various reasons for the failure of all these police operations.

1. From the year 2002

In 2002, the Governor of Kinshasa launched the "Kanga vagabond" (Stop the vagrant) operation. As its name suggests, the main target of the operation was Shégué, the street children mentioned above, who hang around on the public highway, at the market and spend the night under the stars. It quickly spread to other delinquents, including the Kuluna [51].

The violence with which these marginalised people were hunted down provoked strong reactions from human organisations. Once they had been caught, they were brought before a judge very quickly and then sent to prison. The brutality of The operation provoked protests from human rights organisations. The provincial authority was therefore forced to back down.

2. From the year 2003

After a slight lull, the assassination of a senior government official following year (**2003**) triggered a new large-scale operation known as "operation kimia" (peace). This involved a large-scale deployment of police throughout the city. They cordoned off entire neighbourhoods at night and carried out systematic searches. Many Kuluna and criminals from the ranks of the Congolese armed forces fell into their trap and were apprehended. According to some authors, this initiative succeeded in reducing the crime rate. Shortly afterwards, the forces of law and order lost momentum and the criminals came out of the woodwork (Kuna Maba & Mavakala, 2015).

3. The year 2004

The murder of a Belgian priest in Kimwenza, a district on the outskirts of Kinshasa, in **2004** aroused a great deal of emotion and put the police authorities back on the alertOperation Keba" (Be careful) mobilised the troops. Pedestrian and motorised teams organised patrols in the city's outlying districts. The operation fizzled out as soon as the emotion caused by the disappearance of the Jesuit missionary subsided(52).

4. From the year 2013

Seven years later (**in 2013**), the Governor of the city organised a major police operation against urban banditry. It was named "Operation Likofi" (Punch). The aim was to deal a heavy blow to the Kuluna gangs. The town was pacified for a whole quarter, with some Kuluna arrested and others taking refuge in provinces close to the capital. Faced with the irregularities and lack of respect for rights and freedoms in the implementation of this action, national and international NGOs stood up and in turn dealt a major blow to the Governor, who immediately backed down. But the Congolese authorities are not short of imagination in their efforts to extinguish the banditry that is terrorising the town. To make an impression and force the Kuluna to behave themselves, the Ministry of Justice organised mass deportations of arrested Kuluna to prisons in the provinces, suggesting that conditions there were even more inhumane (Shomba Kinyamba, 2015a, p. 39). As always, there was a relative lull. But very soon, the Kuluna who remained at liberty learned that the treatment their compatriots were suffering was not as cruel as they were led to believe. They resumed their work and even took the initiative of recruiting new members.

5. the National Service, year 2020

After a number of criticisms and blunders levelled by certain human rights organisations at Likofi's operating method launched by the Congolese police, the Kuluna phenomenon has resurfaced in the city of Kinshasa. In 2020, the successor regime to the one that initiated the previous operations seems to have found a way of dealing with this barbaric phenomenon, but this time in a more gentle, bloodless way. President Tshisekedi (DRC) has found the Kulunas a necessary workforce for national service. Instead of exterminating them, he prefers to assign them to activities of national interest. He therefore instructed the government to develop the national service created in 1997, by multiplying the number of these centres. In order to find a calmer way of severely re-educating these young Kulunas through community work.

5.1 Failure of anti-Kuluna police action

a. Lack of logistical and strategic resources

The National Police (PN) is one of the archaic and least equipped police forces in Africa's Great Lakes region. It lacks the material and financial resources needed to accomplish its mission. These days, the pick-ups that are supposed to provide police mobility are at our fingertips and in poor condition. In addition, the operational areas of the Kulunas and their places of refuge are sometimes inaccessible by vehicle and require motorbikes to access them, which the Police do not have almost not at apart from of a few motorcyclists who accompany the processions of the authorities.[53] Personal equipment is not regularly made available to them to enable them to take action. The logistics of the Congolese police force extend as far as their salaries, which are the most distressing for civil servants. This means that police officers, being miserly, cannot be effective carrying out their mission with the necessary motivation to track down the troublemakers, including the Kulunas, and ensure the security of the population with self-sacrifice. Without adequate logistics and sufficient motivation. It is one thing to entrust the task of securing people and their property, and quite another to provide the necessary resources. It is also important to remember the strategic challenge of the policy in the fight against Kuluna. It lacks professionalism due to the inadequate training of many police officers. Most police officers have not completed their primary education and are probably not well trained in this profession. Furthermore, it is not out of the question to find among the police officers, former Kulunas, who have no police ethics. Upgrading police officers is therefore a prerequisite for modernising a police force capable of dealing with the contingencies of the society it is called upon to protect.

b. Police complicity with the kulunas

Paradoxically, some police officers are in league with the Kulunas, acting in concert with them and providing them with protection during operations. During night-time operations officially described as patrols, police officers who come across the Kulunas returning from their crimes or who catch them in action do not arrest them, but share the loot with . From this point of view, the police are in a way contributing to the rise of the phenomenon. Aware of this complicity, the Kulunas have no fear of the police, who they know are birds of a feather, but whose fault is that? Without beating about the bush, we can say that the State is at the root of this paradox, because it has failed to ensure that police officers are treated with the dignity they deserve in the performance of their honourable duties.

C. Corruption certain magistrates investigating cases involving the Kulunas

The police and the public often report cases of Kulunas sent to the public prosecutor's office to be investigated and brought before the courts, but which are not followed up satisfactorily because within 48 hours, the offenders arrested are moving around in the same neighbourhoods where they committed the crimes. Clientelism and corruption on the part of certain investigating magistrates are weighing down the work of the police, who appear to be treading water in an old circle, with the result that their operational capacity is being further weakened by the growing power of the Kuluna phenomenon. Similarly, those who, in exceptional cases, can be convicted and imprisoned, do not have the means to do so. are not worried, because the conditions in Congolese prisons are neither intimidating nor re-educating, and the Kulunas leave there more delinquent than they were before they were incarcerated.

Section 4. TOWARDS A NEW RESPONSE

Given the failure of the various police operations listed above, and given the rise in insecurity in the country in general and in the city of Kinshasa in particular, the National Police, being a public service, is supposed to adapt to the new threats facing our country in general and our capital in particular. Given the urgent need respond to the growing distress of the population, we are proposing the strengthening of territorial and local units and the creation of an anti-gang brigade within the national police force. Following the example of other anti-gang units around the world, its mission would be to fight effectively against criminal gangs in the country in general and in Kinshasa in particular. It is only after the creation of this brigade that a large-scale operation can be launched. But to avoid repeating the failures of the past, there are a number of prerequisites before launching this large-scale operation. These prerequisites include good planning; the operation must be well planned if it is to succeed. The brigade will need to be well trained in anti-gang operations, better equipped to enable it to carry out operations successfully, and well remunerated to ensure it is well motivated.

§.1 strengthening territorial and local units

Strengthening territorial and local units is a priority in the National Police's response to this phenomenon. These units play a very important role in ensuring the safety of citizens as they are close to the population and know the realities of every corner of the country in general and the capital in particular. It is appalling to note that these units, which are on the front line against the kulunas, are not sufficiently equipped or trained, which is undermining the National Police's response to this phenomenon. Today, it is imperative that the authorities provide these units with the financial and material resources they need to deal with this growing insecurity. In the same vein, it's worth noting that the territorial and local units are in the front line in the fight against this phenomenon, so the government is supposed to give them the means to do so. Unfortunately, as we pointed out above, these units lack the means to deal with this phenomenon; in some neighbourhoods even, the police officers in these units have taken to the streets for lack of the means to enable them to act when these bandits kill each other. This situation is hampering the fight against this phenomenon, which is on the increase in our capital. That's why we need to reinforce the territorial units in terms of manpower and equipment. Finally, we are proposing the creation of a municipal mobile squadron **(EMM)** at each local police station, support the sub-stations and police stations.

1. From municipal mobile squadron

The municipal mobile squadron is a level one intervention unit of the National Police, responsible for insecurity in a municipality. It will be led by a senior superintendent, assisted by one or more deputies responsible for operations, intelligence and logistics.

A. Mission

The EMM's mission is to combat insecurity in a municipality. It is always expected to be the first to intervene in the event of any act seriously disturbing public order, until level two intervention units arrive on the scene.

B. Training

- Combat sport
- Precision shooting
- Climbing
- Medical resuscitation

C. Recruitment

- First you have to be a police officer,
- It is necessary a certain seniority,
- Be at least 25 years old,

- Pass physical, medical and psycho-technical aptitude .

D. Equipment

- Black fatigues with a Police Nationale, Rapid Intervention Force and squadron crest,
- Personal protective helmet ;
- Gillet by bullet
- Tear gas canister
- Semi-automatic pistol
- Protective shield
- Portable radio
- Electric pulse gun (Tasser)
- Torch
- Pair of handcuffs
- Baton
- Assault rifle

In addition to the EMM, it is important to mention the mobile intervention squadron, which plays a major role in the fight against this phenomenon. The mobile intervention squadron is a level one intervention unit attached to each district police station, with the mission of supporting communal police stations in the fight against crime. To do this, it is supposed to have sufficient resources to carry out its mission, but unfortunately the majority of mobile intervention squads in Kinshasa do not have sufficient resources to carry out their missions.

This situation is hampering the fight against urban crime in Kinshasa. That's why it's vital to provide this National Police intervention unit with the resources it needs.

2. The mobile intervention

A. Mission

As mentioned above, its role is support a police station in the fight against insecurity and the restoration of public order. It is supposed to be headed by a Deputy Commissioner assisted by one or more deputies.

B. Training

See the EMM website

C. Recruitment

See the EMM website

D. Equipment

See those of EMM

Now that we've got that out of the way, let's talk about BRAG.

§. 2 Organisation of the Anti-Gang Brigade (BRAG)

The BRAG is an investigation and intervention unit of the National Police responsible for combating urban banditry. Its senior officer is assisted by two deputies, one responsible for administrative and judicial policing and other for support and management.

The anti-gang brigade will report to the Provincial Commissariat of the National Police.

It consists a :

1. an operations office ;
2. a technical office ;
3. a personnel administration office ;
4. a logistics office ;
5. a health post ;
6. a support squadron ;
7. four intervention squadrons ;
8. an administrative section.

It has a team in charge of administrative policing (patrols, interventions, escorts, reserve policing). A team in charge of the judicial police (judicial police officers, judicial police agents) NB: when the BRAG carries out patrols, rounds or interventions, it comes under the Provincial Coordination of Administrative Police and when it acts within the framework of judicial police missions, it comes under the Provincial Coordination of Judicial Police.

1. Tasks and responsibilities of the anti-gang brigade

1. Ensure that public order is maintained and re-established in areas that are dangerous, at risk or difficult to access;
2. Participate in the prevention and suppression of offences committed by criminal gangs.

A. Ensure that public order is maintained and re-established in areas (dangerous, high-risk and difficult to access)

❖ Article 16.2 of the Organic Law of 11 August 2011 stipulates that one of the ordinary tasks of the National Police is to fight crime;

❖ To this end, in the event of a public order disturbance, the Anti-Gangs Brigade Agents are obliged to comply promptly with any lawful requisition from the competent Authorities.

- BRAG agents maintain and re-establish public order in dangerous, high-risk or hard-to-reach areas, with strict respect for human rights.
- BRAG provides support to the various police stations and sub-police stations within its remit.
- The BRAG can provide support to the Anti-Terrorist Brigade (BRAT) and the Anti-Riot Brigade (BRAE) in the following areas

mutual.

B. Helping to prevent and punish offences committed by criminal gangs

- It investigates the occurrence of one or more crimes committed by gangs and receives complaints from victims of these gangs.
- In the framework of the prevention, it can carry out to awareness campaigns to discourage young people from joining these gangs.

2. Setting up BRAG

The BRAG will be attached to each Provincial Police Station. It will therefore be placed under the authority of the Provincial Commissioner of Police for each province, and each BRAG will be headed by a commander with the rank of senior principal commissioner.

Below is a list of the different BRAGs:

- **BRAG Kinshasa**: attached to the Kinshasa Provincial Police Station
- **BRAG Matadi**: attached to the Commissariat Provincial du kongo Central
- **BRAG Kikwit**: attached to the Mai- ndombe Provincial Police Station
- **The Kenge BRAG**: attached to the Kwuilu Provincial Police Station
- **BRAG Bandundu Ville**: attached to the police station

- **BRAG Lubumbashi**: attached to Haut Katanga Provincial Police Station
- **BRAG Kolwezi**: attached to the Lualaba Provincial Police Station
- **BRAG Haut-Lomami**: attached to the Kamina Provincial Police Station
- **BRAG Kasaï**: attached to the Tshikapa Provincial Police Station
- **BRAG Kasaï Oriental**: attached to the Mbuji-Mayi Provincial Police Station
- **BRAG Kasaï Central**: attached to the Kananga Provincial Police Station
- **BRAG Kindu**: attached to the Maniema Provincial Police Station
- **BRAG Goma**: attached to the North Kivu Provincial Police Station
- **BRAG Bunia**: attached to the Ituri Provincial Commissariat
- **BRAG Bukavu**: attached to the South Kivu Provincial Police Station
- **BRAG Kisangani**: attached to the Tshopo Provincial Police Station
- **The Lisala BRAG**: attached to the Mongola Provincial Police Station
- **Isiro BRAG**: attached to the Haut- Uele Provincial Commissariat
- **Kabinda BRAG**: attached to the Lomami Provincial Police Station
- **BRAG Lusambo**: attached to the Sankuru Provincial Police Station
- **The Boende BRAG**: attached to the Tshuapa Provincial Police Station...

3. Training

- High-level self-defence combat sport
- Precision shooting
- Rock climbing
- Skydiving
- Breaking and entering

- Dog handlers
- Medical intensive care
- Abseiling
- Working in columns
- Discrete approach
- Overcoming obstacles.

4. Recruitment

To be recruited by BRAG, you must :

- Be a police officer for at least 5 years;
- Have already served in a level 2 intervention unit for at least 3 years
- Be under 40 years of age
- At least one good rating in intervention
- Have successfully completed police academy for commissioners and the police academy for deputy commissioners and others;
- Have a basic knowledge of banditry;
- Be ranked in useful order during the theoretical and practical entrance exam (deployment to the operational theatre or during an exercise).

3. Personal equipment

Each police officer in the anti-gang unit must have :

- A pistol,
- Protective helmet ;
- With a truncheon,

- A pair of handcuffs,
- A bullet-proof waistcoat.
- Assault rifle
- Knee, elbow and glove protection
- Glasses
- Balaclava
- Pair of rubber handcuffs

4. Public facilities

- ► Percussion grenades
- ► Tear gas
- ► Helmets for maintaining order
- ► Riot shields
- ► An electrical impulse gun called a Tasser

5. Car fleet

- ► Unmarked vehicles
- ► Patrol vehicles
- ► Off-road vehicles
- ► Vehicles (van)
- ► Troop transport vehicle
- ► Motorbikes

6. How it works

As part of their remit to track down members of criminal gangs criminal known as commonly kuluna on the of BRAG agents can operate in two ways:

Dress

❖ **The BRAG uniform will consist of black fatigues with a national police crest followed by the BRAG crest on the left.**

left and that of the Rapid Intervention on the right

► In uniform for unit support operations

territorial and local (intervention using USVs or, in some cases, ATVs, or using vehicles known as vans)

► Either in civilian clothes, but wearing a blue armband

stamped "BRAG" and also wearing Balitisque helmets and bullet-proof waistcoats operating with unmarked vehicles when carrying out a special operation to arrest a dangerous criminal in the red zones, e.g. in Makala.

► This operation must be a "lightning intervention" lasting a few minutes. minutes at the most.

For night operations, the ballistic helmet must be fitted with an infra-red sight.

7. Means of communication

A police headset fitted with a microphone enabling the police officer to be connected to the officer in charge of the operation and the head of the operation to be connected to command. Or they can be equipped with a ballistic helmet fitted with a radio.

8. Training

Like all police officers, BRAG officers expected to train every day before going on duty. For example, they have to walk and do physical exercises every day. In addition, every 3 months BRAS officers must take part in exercises at the CEP police training centres.

CONCLUSION

As part of our work on ineffectiveness of the national police in dealing with the rise of urban banditry in Kinshasa, we first retraced the history of the national police, saying that the national police had its beginnings in the creation of the public force by the Minister of the Interior of the Kingdom of Belgium at that time. It was made up of two structures, one of which was a military structure responsible for protecting the entire territory of the Independent State of Congo (EIC) against external aggression, and the other a police structure called the Territorial Service responsible for ensuring public safety. When our country gained independence, the territorial service was transformed into the Gendarmerie and then into the national police. Six years after Lieutenant General Joseph Mobutu came to power, it was disbanded to make way for the Zairian National Gendarmerie, and a few years later the Civil Guard came into being. We lived with this system until the late Laurent Desire Kabila came to power through the AFDL. He disbanded the two forces military to create a new police force, the Police Nationale Congolaise, in reference to the rebatisation of the DRC. In the same vein, after looking at the history of the National Police, we spoke in the second chapter of the history of this phenomenon, in which we said that it emerged around the year 2000 through stables made up of leada following the serious deterioration of the country's economic situation and the absence of the State. We also looked at the various causes of this phenomenon, including youth unemployment, drug use, parental poverty, feelings of insecurity and revenge. We then discussed the various police operations carried out against this phenomenon and the reasons for their failure. Finally, we proposed that the government carry out a wide-ranging reform of the national police in the long term and in the short term to create an Anti-Gang Brigade within the national police which will be responsible for tracking down these thugs, but this Brigade will have to be sufficiently equipped to carry out this delicate task properly.

BIBLIOGRAPHY

1. LEGAL AND REGULATORY TEXTS

A. Legal texts

❖ The Constitution of 18 February 2006, as amended by Act 11/022 of 20 January 2011 amending certain articles of the constitution of 18 february 2006 J.O 52 th year 5 february 2011

❖ Organic Law N°11/013 of 11 August 2011 on the Organisation and Functioning of the Congolese National Police J.O 51eme année le 11 August 2011

B. Regulatory texts

❖ Décret-Loi N°002/2002 du 26 janvier 2002 portant institution, organisation et fonctionnement de la Police Nationale J.O 53 ème année le 26 janvier 2002

❖ Decree no. 13/039 of 16 September 2013 determining the organisation and the workings of the Police High Council J. O54 th on 16 September 2013

❖ Decree no. 13 /017 of 16 June 2013 on the organisation and functioning of the General Commissariat of the Congolese National Police J.O 54 ème année 6 June 2013

❖ Decree n°15/026 of 09 December 2015 determining the organisation and the operation of the national police inspectorate J. O56 th year on 9 December 2015

❖ Decree N°15 /027 determining the organisation and operation of the Provincial Commissariats J.O 56th year 9 December 2015

❖ Decree N°042/2002 establishing ranks and insignia within the PNC J.O 43rd year 22 April 2002

II. DOCTRINE

1. Publications

❖Lagrange Marc-André and Thierry Vircoulon, The Kuluna, gangs of the Democratic Republic of Congo, Global initiative May 2021

2. Memory

❖BUGNON Géraldine construction des frontières entre force légitime et violence, Master's thesis in sociology, sociology department

❖KIPASA MAYIGULU Patrick, dissertation on the Kuluna phenomenon and the public arena in Kinshasa, Faculty of Economic and Social Sciences, Politics and Communication, Academic year: 2018 - 2019, UC Louvain

❖Emile Media mbembe, the involvement of Congolese security forces in the development and reconstruction of the Republic of Congo
post-conflict Democratic Republic of Congo, Faculty of Social, Administrative and Political Sciences, University of Kinshasa, 2006 to 2008

❖MEDIA MBEMBE Emile,l'implication force sécurité congolaise au processus de développement et de reconstruction de la République démocratique du Congo post-conflit, faculté des sciences sociales

3. Webography

❖http://www.wikipedia.com "la force publique", consulted on 31 March 2023

❖http://www.afridesk.org/retro-le-colonel-bem-pierre-fwamba the gendarmerie- nationale-zaïroise " consulted on 22 March 2023 at 10:32 am

❖http://wwwFar-maroc. Forum pro. F1 royal moracan Armed Forces : " Armies of the world ": Africa consulted on 04 March 2023 at 11.30 a.m.

TABLE OF CONTENTS

A young kuluna throws a stone

Young Kuluna in combat position

Former kulunas now nation-builders As part of national service S.N acronym

General-Major Jean Pierre Kabwik, Commander of the National Service

Commissaire divisionnaire Célestin KANYAMA former Chief of Police for the city of Kinshasa and current Director of the National Police Schools and Training He was the leader of the Anti-Kulana operation, known as Operation Likofi.

This uniform should be reserved for National Police intervention units in general and the BRAG in particular.

Police officers in territorial and local units should wear this type of uniform in order to differentiate them from police officers in specialised National Police units.

Deputy Divisional Commissioner Blaise KILIMBALIMBA, Head of the Kinshasa City Police.

This uniform should be reserved for specialised National Police units only.

Kolibri 360 GmbH
Ferdinand-Jühlke-Straße 7
99095 Erfurt, Deutschland
produktsicherheit@kolibri360.de

Druck:
CPI Druckdienstleistungen GmbH
im Auftrag der
Kolibri 360 GmbH
Ferdinand-Jühlke-Str. 7
99095 Erfurt